I

LOVE

YOU

From My Heart To Yours

By Gilbert James

Into Thine Hand
4141 NW 39th Ave
Fort Lauderdale FL 33309
www.intothinehand.com

I LOVE YOU

ISBN: 978-0-9841231-2-4

LOVERS CALENDAR

♥*January Is The Beginning Of Each Calendar Year*
♥*Preserve Your Love With Tender Loving Care*
♥*The Month After January, Love Birds, Is February*
♥*Make Sure Your Love Bond Is Strong And Stationary*
♥*March Is The Month That Comes In Third*
♥*Please Speak Your Love To The One Your Heart's Preferred*
♥*April Is The Month To Give Lovers Thrills*
♥*Make Sure You Give Them In Diverse Love Bills*
♥*No Love Decay, Month May Is Not Here To Stay*
♥*Give Love In A Vase And Give Your Heart Away*
♥*The Month After May, Vandal, Is June*
♥*The Month Your Love Cords Should Be Set In Tune*
♥*Take It Or Leave It, We're Now In July*
♥*The Month You Should Die To Let Your Love Fly High*
♥*Month August Like Dust Has Sneaked Upon Our Bust*
♥*Let's Give All That's In Us To Worth Our Partner's Trust*
♥*Stick, Stone Or Timber, We Are Now In Month September*
♥*Let's All Get Together And Make This A Time To Remember*
♥*The Month Of October Has Now Taken Over*
♥*Please Be Thou Sober And So Think Things Over*
♥*Take Stock You Love Offender, We Are Now In Month November*
♥*Irrespective Of Your Gender, Be This Month, A Surprise Sender*
♥*Hi There You Love Pretender, Please Remember, It Is December*
♥*Tough You Have Been Your Love Contender, This Month Be Your Love Defender*

Gift Sender/Receiver Page

From Your:

☐ *Wife* ☐ *Husband* ☐ *Prospective husband* ☐ *Fiancé* ☐ *Fiancée* ☐
Fiancé to be ☐ *Fiancée to be* ☐ *New girlfriend* ☐ *New boyfriend* ☐
The one who loves you the most ☐ *Other:* _____

Print Name: _____ *Signature:* _____

To My:

☐ *Wife* ☐ *Husband* ☐ *Prospective Wife* ☐ *Prospective Husband*
☐ *Fiancé* ☐ *Fiancée* ☐ *Fiancé to be* ☐ *Fiancée to be* ☐ *New Girlfriend* ☐
New Boyfriend ☐ *The one I love the most* ☐ *Other:* _____

Print Name: _____ *Signature:* _____

Dedicated to:

☐ *My love for you* ☐ *Our Marriage* ☐ *Our Anniversary* ☐ *Our
engagement* ☐ *Our engagement to be* ☐ *Our continuing friendship*
☐ *The continuing unity of our relationship* ☐ *Other:* _____

PROHIBITION
This book is intended to be used for the strengthening of the 'single love' relation ship, instead of flirtation! My beloved is mine and I am his: let him feed among my lilies (Sol. 2:16)

PERSONAL LETTER

♥ *My love for you is heated a thousand times the highest*

THE GREATEST LOVE

THE GREATEST
LOVE
Greater love hath no
man than this, that a
man lay down his
life for his friends.
(John 15:13)

THE IDEAL WOMAN

♥She's a lady within a lady
♥She's a heart within a heart
♥She spreads out to give you shady
♥From within her inward part

♥She's a woman of tending caliber
♥She's a vision of sending ranks
♥And her love is like a river
♥That flows within her banks

♥It ascends to the high and mighty
♥It descends to the weak and low
♥In meekness it runs and cites thee
♥Like an arrow thumbed from her bow

♥May the good Lord bless and keep her
♥And supply her every need
♥May His loving wings spread over
♥And protect her cherry seed

Dedicated to Cynthia Scott, whose life has been a living Bible and has reached out and helped countless numbers of needy folks who have come her way, including me (Gilbert James)

THE IDEAL MAN

💣He's the king whose throne is found above life's sky but sends a rainbow to help the dungeon waters rise above life's sea

💣He's the priest who sees farther than the telescopic spy but often appears blind to help the blind to see

💣He's the soldier whose rank is distantly far and high, but condescends to help the broken winged to climb his kasha tree

💣He's the man whose presence demands respect you cannot buy, but is seasoned with a medium that gives comfort to the be and courage to the hope to be.

A tribute to Lt. Leonard Reed Jr., St. Thomas USVI, for being a major milestone in my life's progress (Gilbert James)

DOES LOVE REALLY EXIST?

A Secret Only Know To Those Truly In Love

LOVE

L is for losing oneself in the other
O is overcoming the fear of forever
V is for vowing ones heart to its favor
E is enduring the pains of together

Well, my friends, we approach one of the most misunderstood words in the English language: LOVE. At times we abuse it, at times we accuse it. At times we misuse it, and sometimes we try to refuse it. It is claimed by many but possessed by few. It's a language that can be spoken by all but truly learned by a remnant. It is often consciously and unconsciously misrepresented by its counterfeits such as lust, infatuation, passion, attraction, etc. However, none of these in itself is love or should be substituted for it.

Love is far deeper and of a more noble character than any of these. Though not always recognized or admitted, it is the most precious and valuable treasure that one can ever possess. If you never truly owned any treasure in this world but true love, you are richer than the richest person, with his/her riches in lands and gold, without love. It is more precious than the finest piece of silver or the purest piece of gold. Love is more valuable than the most modern gift of civilization or the most enticing drift of deviation. Love has no price tag. It cannot be bought, neither can it be sold.

Let's reason for a moment together. Have you ever truly been in love? Were you trying to love or were you trying to show love? Does love bring action or is love an action word? Were because you had love or were you loving? Would you say that it's better to tell your beloved that you love him/her or that you have love for him/her? Actually, what I am asking you is whether you see love as a noun or a verb or both? Let's reason a little further; is true love found in the physical, the emotion, the logic, the heart, or all of them? Does true love last forever or for a few years? In fewer words, what is love, where does it live, and how long does it last?

Today's lovers or so-called, find it very easy to use the term: "I LOVE YOU." However, many, if not most of the times, what they really mean is "I LUST YOU." You look very physically attractive. You have appealed to my physical and emotional, and I would like both physiques and emotions to meet. What if that outer beauty were to be marred or distorted severely or that luscious body were to be partly destroyed, could you still, to the same degree, say: "I LOVE YOU?" What if you were deprived or denied the physical encounter because of the other person's personal values until you prove yourself worthy of or qualified to handle the other person's love or total commitment? Could you say to the same degree that you have said before: "I LOVE YOU?" If your answers could not be in the affirmative, you have failed the test of true love. What you have or have had is infatuation: An immediate physical urge for the physical and emotional to meet for immediate gratification. Most likely after that goal is realized, your love that you thought you had would have diminished until you are in need of such physical and emotional encounters again.

Another term that is frequently used by today's lovers is "I FELL IN LOVE WITH YOU." The word 'fell' implies a helpless accident. The word 'in,' combined with the verb 'fell' imply that the person just happens to find himself inside of love without knowing how he got there or actively initiating any steps to get there.

Though true love permeates the entire portion of the human makeup, in its effects, controlling and in a real sense, uncontrollable, it is wise to take note that love operates from within. The physical or the outer portion of the human makeup is simply an instrument used by love to express its true nature dwelling within. It settles for no other place but the central and most vulnerable portion of the human members, the heart. This heart is not referring to where the blood is pumped. The part of the human that is under discussion here is the most vulnerable sector of the immaterial aspect of the human makeup, which is referred to as the heart. Just as love is intangible and immaterial in its true nature, so is the heart that love resides in.

The heart is love's treasured throne. If anything falls when love is a reality, it is the heart. Along with the heart goes the resistance and everything else follows. If falling in love means that after the heart goes, everything goes with it, the statement is well in order. But if the term means that your entire being, especially the physical and the emotions have been spanned by love, without an accurate assurance of its residence in the heart, necessarily, I believe that you are yet to experience true love.

To illustrate this truth let's go back to a statement that the wise man, Solomon made: "LOVE IS STRONG AS DEATH..." (Solomon 8:6). Death is stronger than the strongest person there is. No matter how strong you or any other person is, death will conquer. The strongest person who existed (Samson) was conquered by death. Also the most powerful of eternity, Jesus Christ -- 'LOVE' conquered Him to death.

I would even take this a little further to say that love can be seen as stronger than death because love not only conquered life, the life of God's Son, but the same love conquered Him to death to conquer death (1 Corinthians 15:54-57).

Now, is it wrong to say: "I LOVE YOU OR I FALL IN LOVE?" The aim is to point out that when one says: "I LOVE YOU" which is making love a verb, it should be an expression that is voiced only after complete assurance is arrived at concerning the fact that: "I HAVE LOVE FOR YOU." True love is first possessed as a noun then expressed as a verb. And believe me, if and when you possess love as a noun, you won't have any problem expressing it as a verb. You would not have to try to love your, you would have loved in that you would have possessed love. Either you have it or you don't. To feel or show it, you must have it. If possession is emphatic, expression is automatic.

Saying 'I FALL IN LOVE WITH SOMEONE' is not necessarily incorrect if it is done after unmistaken identification is made of the existence of love living within. It should not be just a submission to the physical and emotional desires without logic or reasoning. Physical and emotional desires arrive very often but only last for a while at a time. Love lives on even when those and all else die or evaporate. True love never ceases (1 Corinthians 13:8).

The real question at hand is, what is the real definition of love? Can it be defined, explained, or only illustrated? Here are some striking questions to consider: How large is love? How wide is it? How about depth -- how deep is love? What about strength -- how strong is it? What about length, how long is it? If you have answers to these questions, there exists serious questions about your possession or perception of real love. If you can truthfully say that your love is immeasurable, then you just might have a chance at true possession or perception.

Love is an invisible but real plant that is only seen by its fruits. Like God, love is never seen, but its existence and effects are unavoidable. The possessor cannot help but recognize its presence as well as its effects.

Now, does love seem like a noun or a verb to you? Should you act love or should you act because you have it? Love must exist as a state of heart rather than a state of mere physical or emotional desires. Love must also be launched from a base of knowledge rather than blind surrender to physical desires or emotions. You should not be trying to love once it is born. If love were born, you could do nothing else but to love. In actuality, once love is existing in your heart, you would find yourself trying unsuccessfully not to show it. LOVE -- you cannot hide it. If you have it for someone, it will burst itself out in your every word and deed.

To attribute love to an external force or entity that enters a person at the point of its conception, whether it is considered to be a living or dead entity, is to ascribe a sense of spookiness or even cultic nature to love. The safest and most reasonable view of the origin or operation of love is that the soil or potential for love is a part of the nature of every human being. Sowing the right seeds and giving it the right fertilization, these seeds will germinate into a real healthy and blooming attribute of the human makeup.

The author sees love as a distinctly living but inseparable entity in and of the human makeup. The intensity and magnitude of its human consumption are dependent on its level of development or how strong and healthy its roots have been allowed to take affect in the person. If the right type and measure of the laws of cultivation are executed, the recipient can hardly help but just becoming more aware of its development.

Love is distinct in that it is identifiable distinctly from the other qualities in a person. In its true character, it is unavoidable. It is progressive in its development to the extent that the more developed it is, the more of a force it is to contend with. This is especially a reality when one tries to deny, or destroy it.

It is living because it be a growing or developing entity in humanity. The differences between the development of true love in a human being and pregnancy are (1) at some point, pregnancy becomes separable while the existence of love is inseparable but suppressible and (2) pregnancy is gender selecting but love is not. However, just as the cells or soil exists within the female to germinate an develop children, so is love in every human.

It is of great importance that I point out here that the true test of love is measured by the level of giving that one produces. "For God so loved the world that He gave" (St. John 3:16). "But God proved His love to us in that while we were yet sinners, Christ gave His life for us" [Romans 5:8]. "Greater love hath no man than this, that a man would give his life for his friend" [St. John 15:13]. If you want to find out if a person really loves you, check to see if that person wants to give to you more than he/she wants to receive or take from you. If that person only wants to take from you or take more than he/she wants to give, then your answer is clear, that person needs to experience a dosage of true love.

Though love occupies the most brilliant as well to the least brilliant of the humankind, love is the most foolish giver in all dispensation. Its logic is the most illogical of all available reasoning. Love sees what no eye can see, hears what no ear can hear, feels what no hand can touch and frees what no key can unlock. Yet, what eyes have seen, love may not see. What ears have heard, love may not hear. What hands have touched, love may not feel. What requires great master keys to open love may not walk into. First Corinthians thirteen, verses four through eight says love suffers long, and is kind. It envies not. It vaunts not itself and is not puffed up. It does not behave unseemly. It seeks not its own and is not easily provoked. It thinks no evil. It rejoices not in iniquity [failure or, wrong doing to or by its object] but rejoices in the truth *"indeception"*. It bears all things, believes all things, hopes all things, endures all things.

Be warned that true love exists forever. The apostle Paul in first Corinthians thirteen and verse eight says that *love never ceases!* It might wither and quail because of lack of proper nourishment or fertilization, but its roots never completely die out.

Love is a delightful and most valuable type of treasure. It is said that you shouldn't try to hold on to God, you should let Him hold on to you; so is love. Therefore, don't give up on your most valuable possession, pick it up again with proper treatment, proper laws of cultivation.

LOVE WORDS TO COURT BY
The Heart Of Love Poured Out

Given
♥ I give myself to thyself
♥ As darkness does to light
♥ I lose myself in thyself
♥ In thee I take my flight

♥ If I had the world of love-choice
♥ I'd lose them all for thee
♥ For dove, I have this one vice
♥ I see no one but thee

♥ Oh yes I learn the language
♥ That dearest love has taught
♥ My dear thou art the sandwich
♥ That's flared to fill my heart

♥ I'll show my love unto thee
♥ From the deepest of my heart
♥ I'll give the love that's due thee
♥ From thee I'll never part

Love's Hidden Treasure

♥ Woven, carved and well put together
♥ Darling, you're my love's hidden treasure
♥ Golden, star of my planet ever
♥ True love knows we're meant for each other

♥ *Love, I dream you in my dreams*
♥ *Sail with you down my love streams*
♥ *You're the light in my love-beams*
♥ *And with you, my cold heart steams*

♥ *One by one they come and go*
♥ *As they each put on their show*
♥ *But my heart keeps saying no*
♥ *No one else can I love so*

♥ *I fore-see us in forever*
♥ *As the truest lovers ever*
♥ *As the ones life's storms can't shiver*
♥ *And the love that severs never*

The Gluttonous Love

♥ *Dear Love,*
♥ *Why couldn't you just say borrow or rent or even lease?*
♥ *Why do you have to say OWN?*
♥ *Why couldn't you just say tomorrow, or day after to morrow, or even the day after?*
♥ *Why do you have to say FOREVER?*
♥ *Why couldn't you just say sorrow, or more sorrow, or even much sorrow?*
♥ *Why do you have to send YOUR ARROW?*
♥ *Why couldn't you just take my first heart, or my second, or even my third?*
♥ *Why do you have to OCCUPY MY INNERMOST*

HEART?
♥ *Why couldn't you just take my thoughts in the morning, or morning and noon, or even morning, noon, and evening?*
♥ *Why do you plague my entire being ROUND THE CLOCK?*
♥ *If there is an answer, I would like to know!*

Earth's Love Angel

♥ *Hi earth's angel dressed in love*
♥ *Who looks like love sent from above*
♥ *But flew away like turtle dove*

♥ *You split my heart before you went away*
♥ *You slit my chart, now I can't find my way*
♥ *I miss my path to love recovery bay*

♥ *My heart is now bleeding, the blood from your love arrow*
♥ *For you it is pleading, please quench my love sorrow*
♥ *No one is succeeding to reach my love marrow*

♥ *Come home my love angel, come live in my love dome*
♥ *Don't roam, my sweet angel, this earth is full of foam*
♥ *Come home my earth's angel, this romance leads to home*

Two Loves

♥ *Put your love in my love*
♥ *Rest your heart in mine*

♥ *Then we'll combine two loves*
♥ *And two hearts inter-twine*

Your Love Attack

♥ *Congratulations, my heart died of your love attack!*

Surrender

♥ *O my darling, I surrender*
♥ *Love's crowned beauty, I break down*
♥ *For my roaring heart you conquer*
♥ *With your mysteries all unknown*

♥ *With your love-wind strong and mighty*
♥ *You have swept my heart away*
♥ *To love-mountain high and lofty*
♥ *Where it now will never stray*

♥ *From the deepest of its deepest*
♥ *Now my heart cries out for thee*
♥ *Make me chiefest that thou seekest*
♥ *That, my love, have I made thee*

♥ *So my honey, please don't worry*
♥ *I will never let you down*
♥ *Take it slowly, do not hurry*
♥ *I will ever be your own*

Streets Of Disaster

♥Take your shoes from off your feet
♥Walk right in and take your seat
♥A force like yours upon my street
♥Has absolutely no disaster to meet

"Daffodil"

♥Are you feeling so distraught,
♥You know not even where to start,
♥To map your true chart,
♥To the rhythms of your heart?

♥As you aim to hit your target,
♥And strain to fit life's pocket,
♥Does sore pain become your jacket,
♥And your veins seem out of socket?

♥Please, my darling, be of good cheer.
♥Face your struggles, do not fear!
♥All the signs so now declare,
♥That your skies will soon be clear.

♥Think of God my darling dear.
♥And remember, I do care.
♥Though your efforts brought you
tears,
♥My love for you, will not wear.

The Cautious Heart

♥My ever going logo is "never make love bet"
♥I never give love go-go, am fearful of its threat
♥I sever any love-line that striveth so to set
♥For fear that it will rewind and leave me just its net

♥Cautiously I travel
♥Carefully I lie
♥Consciously I tackle
♥Contending love cry

♥Hello, says your love-plea, my love, my dove, is free
♥Oh go, cries your love-ship, I'll wait right here for thee
♥No show, crows your whirlwind, my love-wind you won't
see
♥Aglow, mows your garden, for this love grows in me

♥Free? free? asks my poor heart
♥Se! Se! your love pleas
♥Love spaceship! please, don't depart
♥Just wait right there for me

♥Let's go now, dear love-wind
♥Love space-ship waits for me
♥My heart is full of roses
♥Love Garden this must be

The Beauty Within First Beauty

♥ *I'm truly in love with beauty*
♥ *I've always searched for it*
♥ *But then I met you Cutie*
♥ *And was drawn beyond your fit*

♥ *If I were to check first beauty*
♥ *I'd give you triple-A plus*
♥ *But I found in you a beauty*
♥ *That goes far beyond your dust*

♥ *There's a beauty within first beauty*
♥ *For that, I've found in you*
♥ *My love is for that beauty*
♥ *And nothing else will do*

♥ *To you I'll pay my duty*
♥ *To you I'll humbly bow*
♥ *With you I'll sign love treaty*
♥ *With you I'll make my vow*

The One And Only You

♥ *Thanks to who, my, love, for you?*
♥ *Most to you for being you.*
♥ *You were born a little you.*
♥ *Now you're just a bigger you.*

♥ *Only you, my love, are you.*
♥ *Solely, wholly, purely you.*

♥No one else sweet dove, is you,
♥Or can be exactly you.

♥You are truly, truly, you.
♥Not a counterfeit of you.
♥Yes, your body houses you.
♥Not your shadow kid, but you.

♥So, be glad that you are you.
♥And just fall in love with you.
♥Now, please take good care of you.
♥You're the one and only you.

The Turtle Dove

♥In awe I watch you turtle dove
♥And swear you came down from above
♥I watch them as they push and shove
♥To take a hold of you my love

♥My mind thinks thoughts of many sorts
♥That say we'll never come apart
♥But love, I pray deep in my heart
♥That these be part of our love chart

♥My dreams, my dove, are made of you
♥I only wish that they come true
♥And if my dreams of you come true
♥No storm can separate us two

♥I wish we'd never say good-bye

♥But stay together by and by
♥At times, my love, my mouth will try
♥But my heart sure can't tell such lie

♥Every time I look at you, my heart just takes a giant leap
♥Every time I think of you, My love just sinks more inches deep
♥Every time I dream of you, I wish that I could live in sleep
♥Every time I move from you, I feel to just sit down and weep

The Distant Connection

♥Blow me a kiss and I'll feel like tomorrow
♥Blow me a kiss and I'll get by today
♥Blow me a kiss and I'll feel no more sorrow
♥Blow me a kiss and you'll brighten my way

♥Give me your lips and my path you will narrow
♥Give me your lips and my heart you will sway
♥Give me your lips, I'll receive your love-arrow
♥Give me your lips and your dues you will pay

♥Lend me your tongue and I'll see you as my sparrow
♥Lend me your tongue and I'll hear what you say
♥Lend me your tongue and you'll suffocate my marrow
♥Lend me your tongue and I'll come without delay

Duty-Free Taxi

♥*Hi there, my dove and fairest foxy*
♥*Thinking of strolling? please take my love taxi*
♥*Take my love tour, my heart's crowned beauty*
♥*Just for you, I am always on duty*

The Split Heart

♥*I told you to stop*
♥*You still set your trap*
♥*And now you slit my chart*

♥*I was full and complete*
♥*I knew no defeat*
♥*And wow, you sent your dart*

♥*To my heart it took its fleet*
♥*Went through without retreat*
♥*Until it tore me apart*

♥*I rejected you before*
♥*You still tried to score*
♥*Now you split my heart*

The Overcomer

♥*Someone has broken my path*
♥*And I am afraid that my chart reads you*
♥*Someone has soaken my thoughts*
♥*And I parade that my heart sees you*
♥*Someone has taken my heart*

♥*And I am amazed that my cart seats you*

Score

♥*Kiss me honey, kiss me*
♥*If your love is full and sure*
♥*Kiss me honey, kiss me*
♥*If 'tis me that you adore*

♥*Take it honey, take it*
♥*Take it now and score*
♥*Just take it, do not fake it*
♥*Your kiss will take me ashore*

♥*Kiss me honey, kiss me*
♥*Our sweet love, you'll assure*
♥*If your love you now give me*
♥*Of your sweet kiss, I want more*

Awoken

♥*Kiss me, stimulate me*
♥*Kiss me, calculate me*
♥*Kiss me, educate me*
♥*Kiss me, dominate me*
♥*Kiss me, unify me*
♥*Kiss me, terrify me*
♥*Kiss me, multiply me*
♥*Kiss me, satisfy me*

♥*I breathlessly crave your kiss!*

Mouth To Mouth

♥*Put your mouth on my mouth*
♥*Pull me for I am thine*
♥*Lock your spout on my spout*
♥*Until you find my mine*
♥*Press your lips on my lips*
♥*Rest your tongue on mine*
♥*Rub your tips on my tips*
♥*Scrub them to a shrine*
♥*Lose yourself in my-self*
♥*As I'll do in thine*
♥*Store yourself on my-shelf*
♥*Then will we be fine*

Owner Of My Heart

♥*Hi there you mysterious and smart*
♥*I am now in distress, you now rule my heart*
♥*In trying to reject whom its owner really art*
♥*I now must admit, it was yours from the start*

The Phone Call

♥*I phoned my heart and my true love, you were*

there
♥*I phoned my heart and your true sound did not wear*
♥*I phoned my heart and you cried out loud and clear*
♥*Handle me please, with tender loving care*

♥*I phoned my heart and your sweet voice I did hear*
♥*I phoned my heart and you greet me with a cheer*
♥*I phoned my heart and you answered yes I am here*
♥*Please don't drown me with your crocodile tears*

♥*Alone I thought but you cried out do not fear*
♥*Alone I thought just to find out, you were here*
♥*My own I sought but my heart found you my dear*
♥*My own I sought thus to find out, "you're my heir!"*

Dial 000-Care

♥*Hi there, you love in the air*
♥*Do I have to reach you with ten thousand stair*
♥*If you'd only show me that you really do care*
♥*I'll reach you though it costs me gallons of precious tears*

The Width And Depth Of Love

♥*Wider than the ocean, deeper than the sea,*
♥*I wish you and all the world could see,*
♥*That so, my dove, is my love for thee.*

I Will Hold On To Love

♥I May Never Be Able To See You Again
♥I May Never Be Able To Be With You Again
♥I May Never Be Able To Touch You Again
♥But As Long As I Am Able
♥My Love Will Live Till Days Innumerable

Fear Not

♥Hi there you precious and sweet
♥Please take a seat and let our hearts meet
♥Come with your fleet, and make no retreat
♥Forces like yours, can know no defeat

Ruler Of My Heart

♥Ruler of my heart, please sit on your throne
♥Rule as its royal, the owner of its crown
♥Conquer all its bounds, my esteemed, class of renown
♥From the very start, it was there for you alone

Sure

♥There are many things I don't know
♥There are many things I don't claim to know
♥There are many things I don't need to know
♥But there is one thing that I know, "I am in Love with you"
♥There are many things that I don't have
♥There are many things that I don't claim to have
♥There are many things that I don't need to have

♥*But there is one thing that I do have, and that is true love for you*

♥*There are many things that I don't mind losing*
♥*There are many things that I really wish to lose*
♥*There are many things that I need to lose*
♥*But beyond any shadow of doubt, I'd never want to lose you*

Torn Love

♥*On the day I met you, I knew I'd found due love*
♥*It takes just us two and I too have known true love*
♥*They take away you and I am still left with pure love*
♥*They break away two and I am now left with torn love*

The Lovers Creed

♥*Do not get married to a Person*
♥*Personalities are changeable*
♥*Don't get married to money*
♥*Money is fade-able*
♥*Do not get married to sympathy*
♥*Sympathy is reversible*
♥*Don't get married to obligation*
♥*Obligation is burden-able*
♥*Do not get married to infatuation*
♥*Infatuation is disguise-able*
♥*Don't get married to attraction*
♥*Attraction is surface-able*
♥*Do not get married to escape*

♥ *Escape is catch-able*
♥ *GET MARRIED TO LOVE*
♥ *For love is unchangeable, unfadeable, unburdenable,*
♥ *Indisguiseable, capable of great depth, and gives liberty*

"Forever"

♥ *Darling, when I think of your sweet love, I crave the word 'forever'*

Good Old Days

♥ *I remember when I saw you as royalty, entreating me to thy throne*
♥ *And my response was with delight, you were like no one I have known*
♥ *I remember when I saw you as the blooming rose in the midst of my garden*
♥ *And just watching you glow was my sweetest delight*
♥ *I remember when I saw you as the stars of my sky*
♥ *And the light you gave was the only light I craved*
♥ *I remember when I saw you as the wings of my morning*
♥ *And we two would fly away to the land of lovers hills*
♥ *I remember when I saw you as the fountain of ripe honey*
♥ *And your sweet substance was on my heart engraved*
♥ *Oh! if I lose my true love, I would be losing you*
♥ *But I will not lose my true love, neither will I lose you*
♥ *So I will strive to keep my true love and so will I keep you*

The Star Of My Dream

Dear royalty,
♥ *long before I met you, I saw you*
♥ *Long before I found you, I was searching for you*
♥ *Long before I was given you, I had you*
♥ *And long before I had you, I longed for you*
♥ *For you were in my dreams, and you are my dreams*

Expressed

♥ *I often thought of the time when you first said YOU*
LOVED ME
♥ *My heart being so silly, I'd mind others instead of thee*
♥ *I did not take the time to observe then and see*
♥ *It was with great depth that you said YOU LOVED ME*
♥ *Love, I am sorry if I were too rid and free*
♥ *Now, with greater depth, I say: "I LOVE THEE"*

Yester-Time

♥ *The most precious thoughts of yester-time*
are those that are you and me inter-twined

Life's Best Moments

♥ *The two best moments of my life*
are those that I spend with you

and those that I spend thinking about you

Don't Ask If I Adore You

♥*Don't ask if I adore you,*
♥*It is hard to say I do.*
♥*Don't ask if I adore you,*
♥*I've asked the same of you.*
♥*Don't ask if I adore you,*
♥*What silly yes can do?*

♥*I've always blindly craved you,*
♥*Oh, would you say I too.*
♥*I've always tried to show you,*
♥*My heart adores, just you.*
♥*But since you still have doubts too,*
♥*I proudly say, I do!*

Tried In The Fire

♥*My love for you was tried in fire.*
♥*It burnt the fire through, and still lives to love you*

My Wedding Dream

♥*I dreamt that I got married*
♥*To the one my love chooses best*
♥*And then I got so worried*
♥*I almost ruined the zest*

♥*By night I was be-wedded*
♥*To the object of my quest*
♥*When I looked at my bid*
♥*So scared I could not rest*

♥*One night I was divided*
♥*With the one my heart possessed*
♥*And when I saw what I did*
♥*I almost failed love test*

The Everlasting Light

♥*My love for you is an everlasting light that has no Switch*

The Speaking Secret

♥*My love for you I wish to keep a secret, but it speaks so loud, I can't hear anything else*

The Broken Space

♥*My love has a broken spot, only you can join*

Together Forever

♥*Together we'll climb life's ladder*
♥*Together we'll find each other*
♥*Together even when things get harder*

♥Together we shall climb life's mountain
♥Together we shall find our fountain
♥Together even when things seem uncertain

♥Together we shall reach our shore
♥Together we shall make the right score
♥Together even when we are not so sure

♥Together we two shall make it
♥Together we both shall take it
♥Together even when earthquakes hit

Lovers Goodbye

♥Good-bye, my love, am now going away
♥But please be assured I'll be back another day
♥Please, my dove, don't let your heart stray
♥For sure, I am set to pass back your way

♥Don't cry my love, I'm not going to stay
♥I soon will be back to make you happy and gay
♥If you so choose, just put up any tray
♥But never put your heart up for give-away

♥Rely, my love, on me all the way
♥My love for you will never fade away
♥I may stray but my heart will find its way

♥*Back to you, its keeper to stay*

♥*In love my dove I part from you this day*
♥*Wishing and hoping I didn't have to say*
♥*Good-bye my love, am now gone away*
♥*But I sure will be back without delay*

The Unwilling Goodbye

♥*I must say good-bye my love, I know you have to go*
♥*But my heart believed a lie my dove, it really does not know*
♥*I wish to know why my love, it really must be so.*
♥*My love will not die my dove, it just won't cease to grow*

♥*If I should still try my love, just seems like a no-no*
♥*But my heart will not buy my dove, the parts of another show*
♥*To sit down and cry my love, just seems like my only ho*
♥*My heart seems to ply my dove, the arrow from your bow*

♥*I'll see you bye and bye my love, it may be high or low*
♥*Your shadow I can' t tie my dove, or hold it with my woo*
♥*Now don't you be shy my love, just face life with a glow*
♥*On our God rely my dove, His blessings you will sow*

BEFORE YOU SAY "I DO"

Getting Really Personal
Honesty Is Reality. How Much Of It Can You Face Head On?

So you are single, meaning that you are not married? If the answer is yes, so what, but on the other hand, why? Who or what is responsible for this heinous crime of you still being a solo team? Is this your choice? Is it because you are not prepared for the change of status? Are you sure that you are going about it the right way? Most importantly, is this what God wants for you?

In the first place, what is wrong with being single, not being married? You may say that even the creator said from the beginning that it is not good for mankind to be alone. But are you really alone? And if so, whose fault it is? With approximately five billion creatures like yourself on this planet, yea your planet, is something radically wrong if you still find yourself alone? With the perpetual availability of one who is always ready and willing to be your friend, Jesus Christ, can you still blame anyone else, if you find yourself still alone today?

Even society, as it becomes more civilized and developed, tells you that you have to be a little on the insane side if you are of full age and still not married, you respond.

You continue: "Are you fully aware that upon my revelation of my not married status, the obvious question is *what is wrong with me and not with them?*" The natural inclination is that something has to be wrong with me, not the masses.

Getting Really Sober
"Take A Stand On The Facts." The Fiction, Yours Or Theirs, Flush!

Does that make it true? What makes you think that the crowd cannot be wrong? In fact, a careful study of the history of mankind reveals that the masses have been wrong most of the times.

- ✔ It was wrong in the garden of Eden when the entire population of mankind participated in the partaking of the forbidden fruit.

- ✔ It was wrong in the days of Noah when only eight out of the population of the entire world (God knows how many) were right. As a result, they were the only ones who chose to enter the ark and be saved from the world flood.

- ✔ It was wrong in the case of Lot when the big cities of Sodom and Gomorrah became the choice of Lot and his family. Abraham and his family, on the other hand, chose the seemingly "actionless" portion with the presence and power of God in their choice. On that occasion, the same Abraham had pleaded for Lot with the angels of God who were about to destroy the apparently well watered cities of Sodom and Gomorrah with Lot and the rest of its occupants.

- ✔ It was wrong throughout the life of the children of Israel where God had only been able to use a remnant of the entire nation down through its history.

- ✔ The masses have proven themselves wrong in choosing the way of destruction over life eternal.

History shows that it has been wrong in prioritizing, diagnosing and choosing most things that really count. So why should you think that this is the end of the world just because the crowd says that something is wrong with you? Do you realize that the crowd follows the crowd? Are you aware that the crowd cheers with the crowd? Do you know that opportunists can always be bought with a more attractive offer without that offer necessarily being in line with a predetermined mission?

If one chooses to remain single, is that recommended? Can anything possibly be right about being single or becoming of full age and not being married?

Surprisingly, there are many things that are right about being single: In the first place, 'it is good.' ...*It is good for a man not to touch a woman. 2. Nevertheless, to avoid fornication, let every man have his own wife, and let every woman have her own husband. [1 Corinthians 7:1-2]*. The word **ἅπτομαι** *Haptomai* (hap'-tom-ahee) used for touch in the original Greek language which the new testament was written in means to fasten one's self to or be joined to. The concept presented here is that of a union, commitment or a binding agreement.

The inclusion of both genders in verse two of 1st Corinthians seven reveals that both both the male and female are being addressed here.

Therefore a proper interpretation of the passage would be that it is good for a person not to touch {joined or fastened to} a mate but to avoid fornication, let every man have his own wife and every woman have her own husband.

Verse eight of 1st Corinthians seven tells us that *it is good* for the unmarried and widows if they abide as the apostle Paul was (not married). *"I say therefore to the unmarried and widows, It is good for them if they abide even as I."*

Verses twenty-five and six of 1st Corinthians seven say that it is good for a virgin so to be. *"25. Now concerning virgins I have no commandment of the Lord: yet I give my judgment, as one that hath obtained mercy of the Lord to be faithful. 26. I suppose therefore that this is good for the present distress, I say, that it is good for a man so to be."*

Verse thirty-seven of 1st Corinthians seven tells us that if you so decree that you will keep your virginity, you do well. *"Nevertheless he that standeth stedfast in his heart, having no necessity, but hath power over his own will, and hath so decreed in his heart that he will keep his virgin, doeth well."*

In the second place, a single person cares for the things of the Lord more than if you were married. First Corinthians seven verses thirty two through thirty four tells us that the unmarried cares for the things of the Lord, how he/she might please the Lord. But the married cares for the things of the world, how he/she might please his/her partner. *"32. But I would have you without carefulness. He that is unmarried careth for the things that belong to the Lord, how he may please the Lord: 33. But he that is married careth for the things that are of the world, how he may please his wife. 34. There is difference also between a wife and a virgin. The un married woman careth for the things of the Lord, that she may be holy both inbody and in spirit: but she that is married careth for the things of the world, how she may please her husband."*

The "single" [not married] can share a union with God that very rarely is matched again after marriage. I remember a time when I was getting very close to a friend and I got very scared. The reason was that I felt backslidden within my heart just to share the closeness that I had with God with someone else. I felt that I was losing my undistracted union that I had with God before I got so close to this friend.

As a single person, you can accomplish your spiritual as well as life's goals without unreasonable distraction. On reason being... you do not have to have second thoughts about a partner when you are planning to reach your future goals. If you are married, biblically, your spouse comes second to God and first over everything and everyone else. As a married person, you are restricted. You are obligated to your partner and the goals that you can accomplish as partners or as a family.

Do you know how many potential geniuses have eclipsed their future because of silly anxiety or curiosity to say "I DO?" The list is long, and will continue to expand. But the question now is who will be next on that list? Will it be you?

Remember that it was the same aspiration and anxiety, yea, curiosity without consideration to the eminent consequence that got our first mother and father, thus the whole human race into this mess that we are in today.

Does it really worth it to allow anxiety or curiosity, yea, greed to dictate your future? It is not worth it to ruin an entire life's potential in one moment, day, week, month or even year's time.

Getting Really Offensive
"Destroy The Snake Under Your Grass."
You Could Be Protecting The Killer Of Your Fields

So you are still single... and whose fault is it? The world, as well as you, yourself are asking you this question "why are you still not married?" In short, who or what is responsible for this heinous crime of you still being a solo team? Is it because that's what you want or is it not? What you want means that you choose over anything and anyone else to remain the way you are, not married.

If you are this way by choice, you are ranked in a category which very few of the people holding a single status have successfully held. You, in contrast to very few others, can shout it from the house top, proudly, (I hope) "I am this way because this is my choice. I am in control of my personal life or destiny." And you should be commended for having been able to exercise, so far, your power of choice.

Thus, you should not only be aware of, but should be man or woman enough to own up to the fact that you have no one else to blame for your status but you, including the pain and, or gain of such status.

If you are forced to remain this way as a result of rejection, it doesn't roll many points into your corner. It could mean that you have much polishing to do to yourself. Being in this status could mean that you are regulated by the people whom you value as valuable. It is also possible that you allow yourself to be enslaved by them. And believe it or not, it could also mean that your prospects cannot perceive what is true value based on their level of evaluation. If so, this could throw many points in your corner. This would mean that the defect, if not defects, is with them instead of you. This would mean that you should give yourself some credit instead of discredit. It could also mean that you are a jewel and probably were not aware of it. This could also mean that you are ranked in a higher bracket than your prospects. Therefore you should feel honored because you might be too good for them, so to speak. God might have someone better for you.

And just might be, you might be this way because you need to reconstruct your strategy. In the first place, your method of searching might need to be right side up. The biblical strategy is as follows: *Seek ye first the kingdom of God and His righteousness and all these things shall be added unto you [Matthew 6:33]*. This should be understood quite clearly that the kingdom of God is referring to salvation or the new birth. Jesus said that except a man be born again, he cannot even see the kingdom of God. He also went on to show that being born again is the requirement for entering into the kingdom of God {John 3:3, 5}. Therefore, you should first seek to be ready for the kingdom or be born again. Next you must seek the righteousness of God. In short, you must seek after righteous living.

Titus 2:12 says that *"teaching us that denying ungodliness and worldly lust, we should live soberly, righteously and godly in this present world."* To live righteously, we must deny ungodly and worldly lust. And this must come before you search for a mate. Please don't get mad at me, I am not the one who said it, the Bible says it. It is a super great possibility that your answer lies right in this ball park. You should probably play in it some more. You might very well come out scoring greatly.

In the second place, your concept of love might need to be restructured. Jesus   said: *"Here in is the great commandment fulfilled: Love the Lord thy God with all thy heart, with all thy soul, and with all thy mind; and thou shall love thy neighbor as thyself" {Matthew 22:37-38}.* According to this passage, your love should be first directed to God, second, yourself, and third, your neighbor.

This passage clearly tells us that we must first fall in love with God. And if you notice further, you will see that we must love our neighbors as ourselves. Love for ourselves must come before our love for our neighbors. We must first set up a pattern of how much we will love our neighbors by how much we are able to love ourselves.

If we cannot truly and effectively love ourselves, we cannot truly and effectively love our neighbors. Therefore it is evident that second to God, we must first seek to truly and effectively love ourselves, respect ourselves, dream of the best for ourselves, have respect to our needs, treat ourselves with the best, especially some TLC [tender loving care], then we will thus be able to treat our neighbors in the same manner.

Some people love themselves first, God second and others last. Some love their mates first, themselves second, and God last. I submit to you that both of these structures need to be completely restructured. The right structure is God first, yourself second and your neighbors third. The truth is that you cannot truly love you until you truly are able to love God. And you cannot truly love your mate or your neighbor until you truly are able to love you. With this same token, if
you can truly love God, you will truly be able to love yourself. And if you can truly love yourself, you will truly be able to attract and love your present or future mate and your neighbors.

Finally, it highly possible that, your single status is what God wants for you. In Matthew 19:12 Jesus said that there are some eunuchs who were made so from birth. No man but the master has any control over that. This means that God made some eunuchs at birth. That is by His divine providence, not by choice.

The word eunuch does not only mean being barren, not able to have children. According to the different uses in Scripture, it refers to someone who remains without an intimate relationship with the opposite sex.

It also refers to someone who has notable abilities and is totally unattached to anything or anyone who will slow or stop him/her from putting those abilities to full use. Examples of this can be found first, in 2 Kings 20:18 *"And of thy sons that shall issue from thee, which thou shalt beget, shall they take away; and they shall be eunuchs in the palace of the king of Babylon."*

Second, God told Jeremiah in Jeremiah 16:2 that he should not take to himself a wife in that place and at that time. *"Thou shalt not take thee a wife, neither shalt thou have sons or daughters in this place."* Whatever the reason might have been, at least for that time and out of that place he was not to take unto him a mate.

Another example of the use of the word eunuch is found in the book of Daniel 1:9, where Daniel, himself was a eunuch *"Now God had brought Daniel into favour and tender love with the prince of the eunuchs."* I have not found any record where Daniel was attached to any wife or had children. It is evident from the scriptures that he was fully freed of any one and anything that would prevent him from fully carrying out his commissioned conviction or course of life.

AM I QUALIFIED FOR MARRIAGE?

Q: Should a Christian seek for a mate or wait on God to provide one?

A: It Is A Christian Principle To Pursue After What Is Desired That Is Biblical: *[Matt. 7:7] Ask, and it shall be given you; seek, and ye shall find; knock, and it shall be opened* unto you: *[Prov. 18:22] Whoso findeth a wife* findeth a good thing, and obtaineth favor of the Lord. Finders were seekers. *[Genesis 24:27]* And he said, Blessed be the Lord God of my master Abraham, who hath not left destitute my master of his mercy and his truth: *I being in the way, the Lord led me* to the house of my master's brethren.

Q: Is It Unbiblical Or Is It Only Cultural For The Female To Approach The Male?

A: *Ruth Pursued Boaz. Though to establish a biblical principle wasn't the intent of this passage, it is not unbiblical: [Ruth 2:1-13]* And Naomi had a kinsman of her husband's, a mighty man of wealth, of the family of Elimelech; and his name was Boaz. *And Ruth the Moabitess said unto Naomi, Let me now go to the field, and glean ears of corn after him in whose sight I shall find grace.* And *she said unto her, Go, my daughter.* And *she went, and came, and gleaned in the field after the reapers: and her hap was to light on a part of the field belonging unto Boaz,* who was of the kindred of Elimelech. And, behold, Boaz came from Bethlehem, and said unto the reapers, The Lord be with you. And they answered him, The Lord bless thee. Then said Boaz unto his servant that was set over the reapers, Whose damsel is this? And the servant that was set over the reapers answered and said, It is the Moabitish damsel that came back with Naomi out of the country of Moab: *And she said, I pray you, let me glean and gather after the reapers among the sheaves: so she came, and hath continued even from the morning until now, that she tarried a little in the house.* Then said Boaz unto Ruth, Hearest thou not, my daughter? Go not to glean in another field, neither go from hence, but abide here fast by my maidens: Let thine eyes be on the field that they do reap, and go thou after them: have I not charged the young men that they shall not touch thee? and when thou art athirst, go unto the vessels, and drink of that which the young men have drawn. *Then she fell on her face, and bowed herself to the ground, and said unto him, Why have I found grace in thine eyes, that thou shouldest take knowledge of me, seeing I am a stranger?* And Boaz answered and said unto her, It hath fully been shewed me, all that thou hast done unto thy mother in law since the death of thine husband: and how thou hast left thy father and thy mother, and the land of thy nativity, and art come unto a people which thou knewest not heretofore. The Lord recompense thy work, and a full reward be given thee of the Lord God of Israel, under whose wings thou art come to trust. *Then she said, Let me find favour in thy sight, my lord; for that thou hast comforted me, and for that thou hast spoken friendly unto thine handmaid.*

Resulting Fact: From This relationship came Jessie who was the father of David From Whose lineage came our Savior Jesus Christ!

Q: Can A Christian Marry An Unbeliever?

A: *[2 Cor. 6:14]* Be ye *not unequally yoked together with unbelievers:* for what fellowship hath righteousness with unrighteousness? and what communion hath light with darkness? *The biblical answer is no.*

Q: What Are Biblical Reasons For Getting Married?

A: To Avoid Fornication: *[1 Corinthians 7:1-2]* Now concerning the things whereof ye wrote unto me: *It is good for a man not to touch [joined or fasten] a woman.* Nevertheless, *to avoid fornication, let every man have his own wife,* and let *every woman have her own husband.*

A: If You Cannot Contain: *[1 Corinthians 7:8-9]* I say therefore to the *unmarried and widows, It is good for them if they abide even as I.* But *if they cannot contain, let them marry:* for *it is better to marry than to burn.*

A: Those Loosed From A Mate: *[1 Corinthians 7:27-28]* Art thou bound unto a wife? seek not to be loosed. *Art thou loosed from a wife? seek not a wife.* But and *if thou marry, thou hast not sinned; and if a virgin marry, she hath not sinned.* Nevertheless such shall have trouble in the flesh: but I spare you.

A: Companionship And Assistance With life's Work: *[Genesis 2:18]* And the Lord God said, *It is not good that the man should be alone; I will make him an HELP meet for him. [Gen. 2:20-24]* And Adam gave names to all cattle, and to the fowl of the air, and to every beast of the field; *but for Adam there was not found an HELP meet for him.* And the Lord God caused a deep sleep to fall upon Adam, and he slept: and he took one of his ribs, and closed up the flesh instead thereof; *And the rib, which the Lord God had taken from man, made he a woman, and brought her unto the man.* And Adam said, This is now bone of my bones, and flesh of my flesh: she shall be called Woman, because she was taken out of Man. *Therefore shall a man leave his father and his mother, and shall cleave unto his wife: and they shall be one flesh.*

Q: Is A Person's Work Habit A Factor To Marriage?

A: God gave Adam a profession and a job before marrying them [Gen. 2:15] And the Lord God took the man, and put him into the garden of Eden *to dress* it and *to keep* it. It was all the way at *[Genesis 2:18]* that God brought up the subject of a mate. And the Lord God said, It is not good that the man should be alone; *I will make him an help meet for him.*

A: The Person Should Have A Work Habit That Resources The Provision For His/Her Household: *[1 Timothy 5:8]* But if *any provide not for his own, and specially for those of his own house,* he hath *denied the faith,* and is *worse than an infidel.*

A: Working Is A Commissioned Habit From The Bible: *[2 Thessalonians 3:10]* For even when we were with you, this we commanded you, that *if any would not work, neither should eat.*

Q: Is A Divorced Person A Biblical Candidate For Marriage?

A: From The Teachings Of The Old Testament Law: *[Deuteronomy 24:1-2]* When *a man hath taken a wife*, and *married her,* and it come to pass that *she find no favour in his eyes, because he hath found some uncleanness in her: then let him write her a bill of divorcement,* and *give it in her hand,* and *send her out of his house.* And *when she is departed* out of his house, *she may go and be another man's wife.*

A: From The Teachings Of Christ: *[Matthew 19:9-12]* And I say unto you, Whosoever shall put away his wife, *except it be for fornication,* and shall *marry another, committeth adultery:* and *whoso marrieth her which is put away doth commit adultery.* His disciples say unto him, *If the case of the man be so with his wife, it is not good to marry.* But he said unto them, *All men cannot receive this saying, save they to whom it is given.*

For there are *[1] some eunuchs, which were so born from their mother's womb:* and there are *[2] some eunuchs, which were made eunuchs of men:* and there be *[3] eunuchs, which have made themselves eunuchs for the kingdom of heaven's sake. He that is able to receive it, let him receive it.*

Except for fornication here is referring to the engagement period of the Jewish marriage which was the first segment of their marriage. This was legally binding and required an actual process of divorcing to be freed from.

This was the case with Joseph and Mary. Though only espoused or engaged, she was referred to as his wife.

The *Bible portrays them as simply an espoused or engaged couple.* *[Matt. 1:18-20]* Now the birth of Jesus Christ was on this wise: When as his mother Mary was *espoused to Joseph, {engagement} before they came together, {consummation}* she was found with child of the Holy Ghost.

Luke's account classifies them as husband and wife. [Luke 2:4-5] 4. And Joseph also went up from Galilee, out of the city of Nazareth, into Judaea, unto the city of David, which is called Bethlehem; (because he was of the house and lineage of David:) 5. To be taxed *with Mary his espoused wife,* being great with child.

Notice also that *when Joseph was considering the private separation or divorce.* The term *"put her away"* was used as was used in *[Malachi 2:16]* THAT IS A DIVORCE. *[Matthew 1:19 & 24]* Then Joseph *her husband,* being a just man, and not willing to make her a publick example, was minded to *put her away privily.* 24. Then Joseph being raised from sleep did as the angel of the Lord had bidden him, and took unto him his wife:

It is clear that *the Jewish culture accepted the belief that sexual involvements during the engagement* period was considered fornication and not adultery. *[John 8:41]* Ye do the deeds of your father. Then said they to him, *We be not born of fornication; we have one Father,* even God.

A: From The Teachings Of The Apostles

If One Of The Unbelieving Mates Get□s Saved And Received An Ultimatum To Deny Belief In Christ Or Else *[1 Corinthians 7:12-15]* But to the rest speak I, not the Lord: If any brother hath *a wife that believeth not,* and *she be pleased to dwell with him,* let him *not put her away.* And the woman which hath an *husband that believeth not,* and if *he be pleased to dwell with her, let her not leave him.* For the unbelieving husband is sanctified by the wife, and the unbelieving wife is sanctified by the husband: else were your children unclean; but now are they holy. But *if the unbelieving depart,* let him depart. *A brother or a sister* is *not under 'bondage' [being made a slave]* in such cases: but God hath called us to peace.

The apostle Paul confirmed in his epistle to the Corinthians the original {or ideal} concept of the original "two staying together." [1 Corinthians 7:10-11] 10. And *unto the married* I command, YET NOT I, BUT THE LORD, *Let not the wife depart from her husband 11. But and if she depart, let her remain unmarried, or be reconciled to her husband: and let not the husband put away his wife.*

Yet in the same chapter, he permitted the divorced to be remarried [1 Corinthians 7:8-9] 8. I say therefore to the unmarried ἄγαμος *Agamos* (ag'-am-os) and widows, It is good for them if they abide even as I. 9. But if they cannot contain, let them marry: for it is better to marry than to burn.

The (a) added to it gives us the unmarried status. *Note the difference [1 Cor. 7:6]* But *I speak this by permission, and not of commandment.* BY PERMISSION . . . NOT OF COMMANDMENT--NOT BY GOD'S PERMISSION TO ME TO SAY IT: but, *"by way of permission to you, not as a commandment."* Jameison-Faussett-Brown Commentary

I speak this by permission, custom of the more conscientious rabbins, to make a difference between the things which they enjoined on their own judgment, and those which they built on the authority of the law. *Adam Clark Commentary*

Based on Jesus' reference to the term "suffered you" or permission in the case of Moses, it is evident that He was saying that Moses' permission through the writing of divorcement was of the same order. [Matt. 19:7-8] 7. They say unto him, Why did Moses then command to give a writing of divorcement, and to put her away? 8. He saith unto them, *Moses because of the hardness of your hearts suffered you to put away your wives:* but from the beginning it was not so.

Jesus Voluntarily, without any question on the issue by His skeptics, brought up the issue of Moses permission and took issue with it in his Beatitudes [Matthew 5:31-32] 31. It hath been said, Whosoever shall put away his wife, let him give her a writing of divorcement: 32. But I say unto you, *That whosoever shall put away his wife, saving for the cause of fornication, causeth her to commit adultery:* and *whosoever shall marry her that is divorced committeth adultery.*

The only exception that the apostle Paul gives with remarrital implications, is in the case of the unbelieving spouse [1 Corinthians 7:12-15] But TO THE REST SPEAK I, NOT THE LORD: If any brother hath a wife that believeth not, and she be pleased to dwell with him, let him not put her away. 13. And the woman which hath an husband that believeth not, and if he be pleased to dwell with her, let her not leave him. 14. For the unbelieving husband is sanctified by the wife, and the unbelieving wife is sanctified by the husband: else were your children unclean; but now are they holy. 15. But *if the unbelieving depart, let him depart. A brother or a sister is not under bondage in such cases: but God hath called us to peace* ...if he/she departs--that is, wishes for separation. Translate, "separateth himself: *offended with her Christianity, and refusing to live with her unless she renounce it., a* brother or a sister is not under bondage--is *not bound to renounce the faith for the sake of retaining her unbelieving husband.* So according to Deuteronomy 13:6-10 Matthew 10:35-37 Luke 14:26, *the act of exposing the choice of the unbelieving relative to follow another god besides the Lord is like putting that unbelieving spouse to death in the spiritual realm,* as the nation of Israel in the O.T. *The unbeliever does not lie under the same obligation* in the case of a *union with his/her spouse,* as in the case of *believer. Jameison-Faussett-Brown*

This is supported by the charge to the believer in [2 Cor. 6:14-17] 14. Be ye not unequally yoked together with unbelievers: for what fellowship hath righteousness with unrighteousness? and what communion hath light with darkness? 15. And what concord hath Christ with Belial? or what part hath he that believeth with an infidel? 16. And what agreement hath the temple of God with idols? for ye are the temple of the living God; as God hath said, I will dwell in them, and walk in them; and I will be their God, and they shall be my people. 17. Wherefore come out from among them, and be ye separate, saith the Lord, and touch not the unclean thing; and I will receive you.

HOW TO CHOOSE AN INTRIGUING FRAGRANCE

"Published By Permission"

Choosing the right parfum should be a pleasant experience. French fragrances range from the subtly mysterious to the triumphantly exotic.

SOME FACTS ABOUT PARFUM

No one is certain when parfum was invented, but it is known that the ancient Greek Physician, Hippocrates, who lived 400 year before Christ, prescribed it for patients with nervous disorders, presumably feeling that it would calm them down.

Sixty years after her death, the Empress Josephine's bedroom still had the lingering scent of her parfum even the most manly of men, her husband, Napoleon Bonaparte, used cologne constantly as did Alexander the Great and Julius Caesar hundreds of years before him. Cardinal Richelieu, Prime Minister of France in the 17th Century, was so fond of attractive scents that he used parfumed bellows to sweeten the rooms of his place. The ancient Greeks were so anxious to keep their homes fragrant that they used to release doves with parfum drenched wings to circle over the dinner table when entertaining.

YOUR OWN SPECIAL FRAGRANCE

A man choosing parfum for his girlfriend for the first time may not quite know what she likes. A woman who has always worn the same scent may be a bit nervous at trying something new, and a non may be different, about buying cologne for himself.

Today, what a wonderful variety of Parfums there are to choose from. Naturally, you will not wear the same fragrance for every event in your life. You would not spray on the scent to play tennis that you would use for the more subtle atmosphere of the office. Nor, if any work is to get done, would you wear the same fragrance to the office as you would choose for dining romantically by candlelight. Neither would a young-middle-aged lady (and that's the oldest that a woman allows herself to get these days) want to send her baby grandson staggering from her lap because she smells exotically of the Arabian nights, he has not yet heard about, when he is confidently expecting a waft of meadow flowers on a summer's afternoon.

So,... decide on your type and your range of activities and then choose carefully, for you are investing in an aura by which you will be noticed and always remembered, but do not try too many fragrances, or your nose will become confused.

HOW PARFUM IS MADE

Briefly, fragrances are obtained by blending essential oils in tiny parts, fixing them in a "base" and then diluting the blend with water and alcohol. Fine natural oils crame from flowers, barks, balsams, grasses, berries, gums and fruits. The distillation process is extremely complicated to the mature eye, but all you really need to decide is "which of the end products from these exotic mixtures is going to be the fragrance for me?"

Do you know the basic difference between Parfum, Eau de Toilette and Eau de Cologne? Top quality fragrances are composed mainly of oils and alcohol, at five different strengths. In order of intensity: Parfum is the most concentrated and has the longest-lasting fragrance. Eau de Parfum is a little less concentrated. In Parfum de Toilette, the fragrance has been slightly diluted. Eau de Toilette (toilet water) is slightly lighter again; and Eau de Cologne (so called because it was first manufactured in Cologne, Germany) has the lightest concentration of all, as well as being the least expensive.

CHOOSING YOUR FRAGRANCE

Flowery Fragrances: If you like a very dainty scent, select from the FLORAL GROUP which uses delicate blends of flower fragrances such as lilac, rose, and the exquisite symbol of innocence, the gardenia. The great names include Je Reviens, Votre, First, Chloe, Gauloise, Fleur de Fleurs, Oscar de La Renta, Metal Versace, and one of the newest, de Paris.

Outdoor Fragrances: This of course, is for the active or sporty woman,andsheshouldchoosefromtheGREENGROUPwhosecomponents are essences derived from grasses, stems, twigs and barks. Try

Yves Saint Laurent's "Y" Chanel 19, Lauren, Cabochard, Rive Gauche, Amazon or Alix.

Classic Fragrances: Style and elegance are synonymous with these fragrances. Choose from the MODERN BLENDS which are called Aldehydes, after the ingredient that gives them a distinctive sparkle and intensity. Examples include Madam Rochas, Calandre, Cleche, Chanel No. 5 and Miss Worth.

Sensual and Exotic Fragrances: If that's how you feel, choose from the ORIENTAL GROUP which utilizes rare flowers, woods and oils from the Far East such as sandalwood and jasmine   Try   Opium, Cartier, Bal a Versailles, Jean Patou 1000, Femme, Ivoire, Mystere, and Shalimar. You will exude sensuality.

Sweet and Spicy Fragrances: If the lighter parfums are for you, choose from the FOUGERE GROUP, and again get advice from the experts as to whether the citrus, woody and herbal tones, or the sweet and spicy with a little sandalwood and oakmoss is right for you. Experiment with Miss Dior, Yendi, Vanderbilt, and Albert Nipon.

Men's Fragrances: Parfums and colognes have long been as much a part of life for men as have clothes and jewelry. The famous warriors of the ancient world, like Alexander the Great, Julius Caesar, and Mark Anthony, were noted for their use of parfums. During the French Revolution, Napoleon was renowned for his constant use of cologne. Many great lovers in romantic history used parfums for allure.

Index

Index

W

Y

Other Books By Into Thine Hand

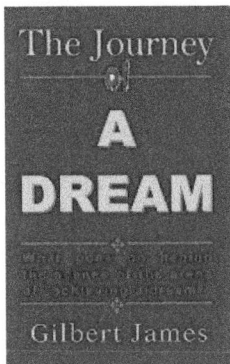

The Journey of A DREAM

Gilbert James

The Journey of a dream is like the road that you travel daily. There are other commuters who are both duly traveling from their departure to their destination and have equal rights to that same terrain as you do. Some will arrive at their destination as intended and some will join the list of casualties. What will make the difference for the list of successful arrivers?

Before You Say I DO

Marriage is a beautiful venture which should also be a beautiful adventure. However, too often we approach the path into marriage passively to realize sooner, rather than later, that we are actively on a path to undo what we now see as something we didn't create. Oft times we are right. "We" did not actively create that bond. Our emotions and anxiety created it for us. We ask ourselves if we were really sober during what should have been the period of examination and confirmation, and the truth is that we probably weren't. We were intoxicated with the bonds of emotion and anxiety. We have effectively allowed ourselves to be led, with our consent, by the person that we read into being the ideal and not who the person really was. We really did not know 'the person.' Before you look back and regret, attack it directly in its pre stage, rather than in its post stage. Be up on your p's and q's during what rightly is the period of dual examination of yourself and spouse "to be." Make sure that you know who 'you' are and your spouse 'to be' is before that grand occasion, and you are indeed giving and marrying that person. Make sure that your standards have been met and vice versa. Most of all, make sure that God's standards are met.

I L♥ve You

From My Heart To Yours

♥Perfect for courtship and the recently engaged

♥Will spice up the long existing relationship

♥A stand alone gift item

♥Add spice to your love letters

♥Share on a one and one encounter

♥A gift from lovers to lovers

♥A gift from family or friend to a young couple

♥Your local flower shop item

Visit www.intothinehand.com for Into Thine Hand's webazines, directories and other products. You can also find our books at your favorite online or local book sellers.

www.ingramcontent.com/pod-product-compliance
Lightning Source LLC
Chambersburg PA
CBHW071024040426
42443CB00007B/925